The 3-Ships of Success

THE 3-SHIPS OF SUCCESS

The Powerful Connectivity of Three Tenants of Business

MacArthur Burton

iUniverse, Inc.
Bloomington

THE 3-SHIPS OF SUCCESS
The Powerful Connectivity of Three Tenants of Business

Copyright © 2009, 2013 by MacArthur Burton.

All rights reserved. No part of this book may be used or reproduced by any means, graphic, electronic, or mechanical, including photocopying, recording, taping or by any information storage retrieval system without the written permission of the publisher except in the case of brief quotations embodied in critical articles and reviews.

iUniverse books may be ordered through booksellers or by contacting:

iUniverse
1663 Liberty Drive
Bloomington, IN 47403
www.iuniverse.com
1-800-Authors (1-800-288-4677)

Because of the dynamic nature of the Internet, any web addresses or links contained in this book may have changed since publication and may no longer be valid. The views expressed in this work are solely those of the author and do not necessarily reflect the views of the publisher, and the publisher hereby disclaims any responsibility for them.

Any people depicted in stock imagery provided by Thinkstock are models, and such images are being used for illustrative purposes only.
Certain stock imagery © Thinkstock.

ISBN: 978-1-4759-6756-2 (sc)
ISBN: 978-1-4759-6757-9 (ebk)

Printed in the United States of America

iUniverse rev. date: 02/11/2013

CONTENTS

Dedication vii
Acknowledgement ix
Introduction xi

The Read 1

Chapter 1   Leadership 3
Chapter 2   Followership 11
Chapter 3   Relationship 17
Section 1 Review 20

The Need 23

Chapter 4   Leadership 25
Chapter 5   Followership 30
Chapter 6   Relationship 37
Section 2 Review 43

The Seed 45

Chapter 7   Leadership 47
Chapter 8   Followership 53
Chapter 9   Relationship 58
Section 3 Review 65

Final Thoughts 67
An Invitation 69
A few things about the author 71
References 73

DEDICATION

I dedicate this book to my loving, supportive wife Gail Burton, who gave of her time, talents, and expertise so unselfishly to aid me with this project. Also, to the many outstanding men and women I have been fortunate enough to have touched my life in some positive way. The relationships we established were formed in waters so deep, neither years nor miles have been able to change their course.

Nothing is more challenging, demanding, frustrating, or rewarding than dealing with people, either as a leader, follower, or through some type of relationship. People are interesting, engaging, disappointing, surprising, and even more. There is no magic formula for dealing with people, just certain, proven ground rules for successful associations.

Although it took some time to realize it, these ground rules are effective in both professional and personal relationships. Simply stated, just treat people like you want to be treated, and most often, things will turn out fine.

ACKNOWLEDGEMENT

To my daughter Jerrisha Sterling, for her outstanding work on the cover design and graphics for this book.

To my daughter Crystal "Mick" Stradford, for her constant encouragement.

To my daughter Jennifer "Rudy" Stringer, who always keeps me thinking with her quick wit and insight; the world is truly your oyster. Seize it!

To my sisters, Leslie, Mable, Carol, and Valeria, always in my corner.

To my late aunt Willie Mae Agnew. I never knew missing you could hurt so much.

To the crew of the 4th Ship, Tony G and Janet, Ike and Tamera, Harry and Karen, Frankie and Linda, Johnny and Nancy O, Tyrone, Skip and Gloria, Flynn, and Dianne, thanks for sailing with me on the Friendship!

INTRODUCTION

In 1492 when Columbus sailed the ocean blue, he did so with three ships. The Pinta, the Nina, and the Santa Maria are almost as famous as Columbus himself. Each ship had a specific purpose, a mission. It took the three ships working in concert with each other to ensure a successful voyage of discovery.

Today, the appeals of business are numerous and take many different formats. Corporate business, Sole Proprietorship, Limited Partnership, Corporation, Limited Liability, and entrepreneurs all address the different forms of business opportunities in the world today. No matter which format is chosen, each provides a continual challenge to master the waves of success aboard three ships. The waters are turbulent, and only the best learn to navigate these waters successfully and survive long term. Business is a science, an ever changing science that requires years of continual study and adaptation to ever changing times.

It is amazingly hard to turn a ship in a different direction once it reaches a full head of steam. People are like that, too. If you wish to turn them in a direction of your choosing, it is better to start early, before they get a full head of steam. That's why I think it is absolutely critical that leadership is very meticulous in selecting members for the followership. You cannot afford to have people represent your company with an attitude of indifference or disdain. I know this may sound hard, but if they are not a good fit, then don't select them. As Chet Holmes states in his book, *The Ultimate Sales Machine*, "Use challenge and rejection when hiring sales staff. Superstars will fight back." Those who don't fight back ... well, that's how you separate the wheat from the chaff. The most effective way to gain success in business is to be successful in communications, especially in communicating with prospective followers about expected standards.

Although difficult to master, it is a simple concept; listen to the people, talk with the people, serve the people, in *leadership, followership, and relationships*. If either of these three is missing, the concept is degraded and success in business will be short lived. For those who embrace the science of business and focus on the simplicity of the concept, the treasures of the sea of business and your personal life will be great, and continuous.

It doesn't take very long browsing in a bookstore to realize there are thousands of books on leadership. And, while the term *followership* may not be quite so common, books on what it takes for workers to improve their status in the workforce are also fairly common. Relationships, in terms of business, have also been covered quite extensively. What is harder to find is having all three topics tied together in one book that deals with being successful. This, to me, is strange because to talk to one without the others is a disservice to the one.

There is an old American axiom that business is business. The most important aspect of success in business is how it is conducted. Business philosophies are as numerous as apples on a tree, but there is one truth; to be successful in business you must know how success works. There are three ships of success in any business; *leadership, followership,* and *relationship*. Each ship has its own unique set of characteristics, and must be understood. The best way to understand is to pick a ship, get aboard, identify a problem, and then define a solution.

Columbus epitomized this concept for me. For him, leadership was important and had to be recognized as such. To that end, he selected the Santa Maria as his flagship. It was the largest ship, and the one he personally sailed on. It also carried the most cargo and the most people (crew). Although the Pinta and the Nina were smaller, they were both critical to the success of his mission. They often sailed in the wake of the leadership, but both were faster and sailed over difficult waters easily. They carried less cargo, but their greater value was in their ability to go places and do things the leadership could not.

Leadership, for whatever reason, seems to draw most of the attention. Perhaps this is because it is easier to identify the head than the body. Leadership is an art, and takes many different forms, such as autocratic, democratic, charismatic, laissez-faire, and well, you get the idea. In fact, there are ten recognized styles of leadership. Each can be used independently, although most often they are used in combinations. Each style is a tool used by leaders in providing directions, focus, and purpose in the <u>control</u> of people, money and facilities. Leaders provide the vision and establish unit goals and direction for middle managers and front line workers. Once the *vision is conveyed* and direction is identified, leadership ensures managers implement *tactical* (day-to-day operations) plans to make certain the goals of the unit are met. Without strong leadership at the helm, the vision loses focus and the ship of success gets off course.

Leadership is about knowing the business, knowing the people in business (both internal and external), and knowing the customers. Leadership requires strong communications skills and the ability to create an atmosphere of success. Leadership knows that *communication is the one job that cannot be delegated*. It is about helping others fulfill their needs. Leadership success is tied directly to the number of people the leader can help.

Although it does not command the same degree of publicity, **followership** is every bit as important as leadership. It is the follower who is the true face of the company, the "first contact" with the customer. Followership, like leadership, is an art. It requires open communication with leadership concerning the company vision, expectations, and job description. Additionally, a good follower must make the effort to project a favorable image. This is not to say you should seek favors (suck up), but rather use proactive tactics (being supportive, respectful, competent, and dependable) versus defensive tactics (constantly making excuses and apologies). Always remember that everyone, including followers, has a "circle of influence." How you use that influence determines who will be drawn into your circle. The more positive the influence, the more you expand your circle. This is crucial in developing customer relations.

The importance of good followership cannot be overstated because, let's face it, there are so many followers. Because of that, one of the most important items for a good follower to learn is his/her value to the success of the business.

The third ship, absolutely essential to any success, is **relationship**. It is through relationships that interactions are established, sustained, and either grow or die. Relationships must be established internally and externally for the health of the business. The two pillars of support in any relationship are *trust* and *respect*. The lack of, or violation of either one can cause irreparable damage to the relationship.

So how is it that the paths of these three ships cross? The ultimate landmark of each ship is the customer. I once read that the provider does not determine the rules, the customer does. Throughout this book you will see how each ship is on a course charted toward the customer. With over thirty-five years in customer service, I still discover new and exciting things about customer service and the ships that deliver to the customer every day.

In Chapters 1-3, a discussion on the meaning, "the read," of the three ships is provided. Specifically, in Chapter 1 we will look into the important elements of leadership... not in terms of style, but how leadership works in relation to the customer. In Chapter 2 we take a similar look at followership rules, responsibilities, and impact. Chapter 3 we take on relationships, both inside and outside of the business.

Success requires skillful negotiation aboard each of these three ships. Chapters 4, 5, and 6 will demonstrate through "the need" how each ship is dependent, interdependent, and independent of each other. Chapters 7, 8 and 9 deals with the components of success, "the seed," as it relates to leadership, followership and relationships. So strap on a life vest, and get ready as we say *Ship ahoy*, and set sail on the sea of success!

You paid your passage; I hope you enjoy the ride.

THE READ

In this section, The Read, we discuss read in its basic meanings; to look at carefully so as to understand the meaning of (something written, printed, etc.); to comprehend or interpret the meaning of (gestures, movements, signals, or the like); to make out the significance of by scrutiny or observation. The tools we need to be successful are all around us every day; if we only read the signs aboard the three ships; leadership, followership and relationship.

CHAPTER 1

Leadership

"Not everything that counts can be counted. Not everything that can be counted counts."
—Albert Einstein

Leadership is about character; period, dot. One of the most important questions I've ever heard regarding leaders and what they should ask of themselves is, "If my character was for sale, would I get full retail value or would I have to sell at discount?" Of all the leadership traits that can be counted, character is right at the top of the list.

Leadership is about knowing what counts, focusing only on what counts, and ensuring your people know and focus on what counts. In his "in-your-face" style, **Larry Winget**, the pit-bull of personal development emphatically states what leaders must do: "Don't measure activity. Measure accomplishment. It doesn't matter what people do as much as it matters what they get done." Bottom line here is only *results* count. Not good intentions, not how many hours were put into the job, or what you *thought* the customer wanted. If the results were not *what* the customers wanted, *when* they wanted it, *how* they wanted it, then the leader's *ship* did not come in. In other words, all that activity counted for nothing.

So how does leadership increase the odds of successful accomplishment? By providing a clear vision, acknowledging understanding from workers and clearing up any ambiguity, and providing the necessary training employees need to fulfill customer expectations. *Leadership must be its own lighthouse*, illuminating the way for followers and ensuring the goal of success is clearly visible in the distance. Focusing light on a shared vision, ensuring understanding of and commitment to successful processes, and empowering others to act are but some of the challenges of leadership.

Let me lower the sails for just a moment to clear up a common misconception. Many people believe there is no difference between leaders and managers; not true. My friend Sandy defined what he believes to be major differences between leaders and managers, and I agree with him and will share them here. Sandy stated, "A manager administers, a leader innovates; a manager maintains, a leader develops; a manager relies on systems, a leader relies on people; a manager counts on control, a leader counts on trust; the manager does things right, the leader does the right things."

Five Leadership Imperatives

Five imperatives the leadership must stay on course with are:

1. **Make it so, and make it known.**
   Leaders must develop a promise that is simple, concise and easily understood by members on both the followership and the relationship.

2. **Give the customer a reason to remember to come back.**
   Today's business atmosphere is one of very low customer expectations and suspect. If you want to establish a lasting relationship, you must exceed customer "suspectations."

3. **Maintain your integrity.**
   Deliver what you say you're going to deliver, the way you say you're going to deliver it, when you say you're going to deliver it.

4. **Stay fresh.**
   Review your service standards regularly and update as needed. Remember, the market constantly changes; you must change to meet the market demands.

5. **Maintain buy-in.**
   Continuously update your team on modernized service standards to obtain their support or hear any concerns they may have regarding the new standards. Remember, team work makes the dream work.

> "Say what you mean, mean what you say, but don't say it mean."

But to be truly successful in leadership requires development of one specialized skill—listening. In the *Business Week* best-seller, *The Leadership Challenge, third edition* by **James Kouzes** and **Barry Posner**, they speak of the importance of listening with your eyes and your heart. They point out that, "learning to understand and see things from another's perspective—to walk in their shoes—is absolutely crucial to building trusting relations and to career success." In other words, listen to others to learn what is important to them, provide to them what is important to them, and you will build a trusting relationship to pave a course to success.

Personal connections are a must in business, and are built through trust. Personal connections establish relationships, cement relationships, and keep relationships afloat. If you want to truly build a relationship, take the focus off of you (selfish) and put the focus on the other party (concern). How do you do this? L-I-S-T-E-N!!!

That's how you discover their motivation, their passions, desires . . . their fire. Trying to convince someone to do something they don't want to do is like trying to push a string; it doesn't work very well. Put more of your energy into finding out what they want to do, what they need, and why. The best way to do this is by listening.

No Fear

Leaders must be fearless, in their dealings with followers and in the face of possibly being fired—especially when fighting for what you believe in. Leadership is about making the tough decisions, even when they are unpopular. This is no easy task. Most people have no problem taking credit when things go well, but look for somewhere to place the blame when things go badly. In leadership, whether smooth sailing or choppy waters, leaders must stay the course. Former Secretary of State **Colin Powell** said, "Good leadership involves responsibility for the welfare of the group, which means some people will get angry at your actions and decisions. It is inevitable—if you're honorable. Trying to get everyone to like you is a sign of mediocrity. You'll avoid the tough decisions, you'll avoid confronting the people who need to be confronted, and you'll avoid offering differential rewards based on differential performance because some people might get upset." And he's right! No one likes to hear that they have an ugly baby, but remember, leadership is about character. If the baby is ugly, it's not going to get any better looking by not addressing it.

Leadership is about setting standards. Emphasize positive, personal appearance at the very beginning, in the training program. Letting followers know what you *expect* early on will earn you *respect*, and quiet many problems when it is time for you to *inspect* and document performance. Early, effective training and adherence to standards lead to early, productive followers. And listen to followers early on to ensure they understand and are willing to comply with company standards.

Leadership, then, means being not just a good listener, but an *effective* listener. Effective in finding what is of value to the followers and the customer, and then providing the product or service that satisfies that perceived value. This is no easy task for the leader. In today's environment, it is unfortunate but true that mediocrity (i.e., mediocre; providing only moderate ability or effort) has replaced excellence as the standard in customer service. The true leader will not allow his ship to get caught in the undertow of mediocrity. The true leader unfolds the sails of trust, respect, and effective listening to navigate the waters of today's success.

> "A leader is someone you choose to follow to a place you wouldn't go by yourself."
> —Futurist Joel Barker

> "In the past, the leader was the person who came up with the right answer. In the future, the leader will be the one who comes up with the right question."
> Peter Drucker
> Father of Modern Management

Knowledge versus Skill

Which is more important, knowledge or skill? It's like that age old question which came first, the chicken or the egg. Both are important, but on weight, which is more important? Academia will tell you that knowledge is power! I rebuke that slightly, in that knowledge itself is not power, but what one does with knowledge can be powerful. Like many of you, I have known my share of educated derelicts; lots of knowledge but little enthusiasm or tolerance for work.

This is not to say that knowledge is a bad thing. Knowledge is a must to get a quality product. However, to be an effective leader, skill is required on many fronts. Lack of solid leadership skills can have a devastating impact on an organization. It takes skill to gain the support of followers and get them moving toward that common goal. It takes skill to tell, sell, and propel the vision of the company, and gain buy-in from followers. It takes skill, when negative events impact on morale outside of the leader's control, to encourage followers to hang in there; things will get better.

Donna applied for and was accepted for a director's position with a new agency. This position is both a promotion and carries supervisory responsibilities. Donna has never supervised before, but is very knowledgeable as a logistician and feels she is more than qualified. Besides, she is ready for a change because her co-workers have always been jealous of her knowledge and full-speed-ahead attitude. A change of environment was just what she needed right now. She would get an opportunity to really showcase her knowledge and make sure her team did just what she said the way she said it; no questions.

It wasn't long before things began to unravel. Donna's team was not only knowledgeable, but heavily experienced at their jobs. She was unprepared for her followers to be just as knowledgeable (if not more so) than she, or to present sound arguments to some of the instructions she was providing. Questions such as, "If we do it this way, will we not lose the opportunity to capitalize over here? Why would we want to move property from here now, when there is an emerging mission projected within a matter of months?" These questions were causing her to lose both patience and her temper with her followers, and ultimately their support. She began to demand reports and refuse to justify her position on different matters, but they were viewed by followers as building a bridge to nowhere. Within a year, two highly respected followers had taken jobs elsewhere, and others were spending hours (some during the work day) on USAJOBS desperately seeking a way out. Donna's knowledge wasn't saving her, and her lack of leadership skills was sinking her.

At this point I think it is important to identify a concept I call the pivot principle. There are going to be times when circumstances dictate a pivot from being a leader to being a manager. Although many think the two terms are interchangeable, there are distinct differences. A manager is a person who controls and manipulates resources. You can manage supplies, you can manage a checkbook, and you can even manage a work group. But leadership is an art. Some even go so far as to say it is the art of influencing others in the attainment of a desired result. Leaders and managers can be the same person, but knowing when to pivot from a leader to a manager is a learned skill in itself.

Skill, as important as it is in a leader, is not a readily apparent asset. It is extremely hard to spot until it is put to the test. An old law (at least it ought to be a law) of business states that time will either promote you, or expose you. All too often, individuals are placed in leadership positions based on knowledge and years in the business. Many times they have no supervisory experience, have never led a team anywhere except to a conference room or cafeteria, and find themselves thrust into senior level director positions. They are not ready, and it is not long before the people working for them know that they are not ready. They are undone by their own deeds ... they are exposed.

Even worse is the leader who either doesn't realize or refuses to recognize the fact that he/she lacks the skill, rather than acknowledging the shortcomings to his/her staff and requesting both patience and assistance. Most times, followers will both appreciate and assist if you come to them correct, but nothing will lose their support faster than poor decisions born of arrogance. Instead of looking at the chicken or the egg, maybe we should be looking at another thought I've heard on the ham and egg comparison. With the ham and egg, you know the chicken is involved, but the pig is committed. In leadership, you're not only expected to be involved, you have to be committed.

The Post Turtle

> *"Behold the turtle. He makes progress only when he sticks his neck out."*
>
> —James Bryant Conant

Here's another little story on leaders I want to share with you. In my military travels, I spent some time in big Cheyenne, WY. Cheyenne is a big, open territory with miles of ranches, range land and highway. I worked a few years on the Frontier Committee for the Frontier Days, the biggest rodeo in the US, also known as the Daddy of 'Em All." I had the opportunity of meeting some great folks, including some of the best cowboys and biggest liars in the world, but all in good fun. While there, I heard stories about everything from antelopes to jack-alopes (a story for another time), but most interesting of all was a very enlightening story about the post turtle.

An old rancher is talking about politics with a young man from the city. He compares a politician to a "post turtle". The young man doesn't understand and asks him, "What is a Post Turtle?"

The old man says, "When you're driving down a country road and you see a fence post with a turtle balanced on top, that's a post turtle. You know he didn't get up there by himself. He doesn't belong there, he can't get anything done while he's up there; and you just want to help the poor, dumb thing down."

Some leaders are like the old story of the post turtle. You look at them in wonder, perplexed about how in the world did they get up on that leadership post. You can tell from their management, speaking, and people skills (or lack of them), that they didn't get up there by themselves. They have no vision, no plan, and as we use to say in another of my previous employments, his idea of leadership is simple; to pee on the fire burning closest to you. He doesn't belong there on that post. He can't get anything done while he's up there, so he is dependent on those around him to keep the ship afloat, and is not bashful about taking the credit for the work of his staff. And even though you may be frustrated and upset initially, after a while, you just want to help the poor dumb fellow down.

American public speaker Jim Rohn said, "If someone is going down the wrong road, he doesn't need motivation to speed him up. What he needs is education to turn him around." When I see folks promoted into positions of leadership that they are clearly not prepared for, I have a similar but different philosophy. If you're going down the wrong road and receive motivation to speed you up, all you will accomplish is arriving at the wrong place faster.

Recognize and acknowledge your limitation. Take actions to get the training, help, and mentorship you need to be a successful leader. The leader who takes the initiative to do these things will greatly reduce the chances of being known as a post turtle.

The Read On Leadership Summary

The Read on Leadership is that leadership is heavily dependent upon the leader's ability to communicate, in the various communication forms. The leader must be aware that non-verbals often gives off more information than their spoken word, positively and/or negatively. Communicating is a two-fold process, where listening is every bit as important as speaking. A leader is hired to get results, and the best way to get results is to be a great communicator. To truly become better at leadership, become a better you. Author Napoleon Hill said, "One goes ahead, stands still, or goes backwards in life." There are many facets of successful leadership, with communications being high on the list. The leader who gets ahead is the leader who continues on the path of personal development.

CHAPTER 2

Followership

"It's not important what we do, but it is absolutely important to treat what we do importantly."
—Actor Kevin Costner

In my book "***Management Out of the Blue***" I ask the question, "Who is more important, the leader or the follower?" A hard question, but fair. The follower is extremely important to any success. Why? Another observation from my book states, "When customers come into your shop for service, who do they have first contact with? One of your followers, right?" That first contact is either a deal maker or a deal breaker.

Followership must sail the waters of competency. To be a good follower, you must know-your-stuff! To do this requires taking advantage of every business offered training opportunity, i.e., classroom, seminar, computer based, or one-on-one training. Additionally, you must take the personal initiative to stay proficient in your field, even if it is only a temporary position.

The 4-Rs

On the ships of success, everyone has a role, and everyone must know their role and believe that they bring value to the business. This value is defined in four unique areas; **responsiveness**, **reliability**, **relationships** (which we will cover later), and **results**. Responsiveness, the first of the 4Rs, speaks directly to followers reacting or responding to customers. The best response comes through a shared vision. If followers believe in the vision of the business, they respond to others in a positive light. There is a Japanese proverb that states, "Vision without action is a daydream. Action without vision is a nightmare." If you observe customer service actions by followers without buy-in to the company vision, what you normally see resembles a nightmare.

However, when there is buy-in to the vision, the results are totally different in a very positive way. Recently I was on a business trip to Las Vegas and had one of these rare, positive experiences. The flight was heavily booked, running a little late, and many of the passengers were visibly frustrated as they boarded. And then it happened. The lead flight attendant's voice filled the airways. "Good morning ladies and gentlemen and welcome aboard Southwest Airlines flight 2872 to Las Vegas. This is a no complaints airline, and that call button over your head also acts as a passenger-eject button. This is also a non-smoking airline, however if you feel the need to smoke during this flight we have set up chairs on the wings of this plane to accommodate you. If you elect to go out for a smoke you will also be featured in our flight movie, *Gone With the Wind*. Also know that our call button means absolutely nothing to us if we are on our union break. Should there be a sudden change in cabin temperature, air mask will drop from the ceiling compartment. There is to be no holding on to the person seated next to you . . . unless they are really, really good looking! If you are a parent traveling with children, please put your mask on first, then help the child. If you are a parent traveling with two children, I am truly sorry, but you will have to decide which one has the most potential. At this time, please pretend to give our crew your attentions as we go over the safety features of this aircraft."

Does this sound like buy-in? The laughter and applause were thunderous. The mood of the entire plane was changed. That's the success of followership. Followers take care of the day-to-day running of the business—focusing on providing a positive experience for the customer. The lead flight attendant above was in very familiar, comfortable waters, and providing a positive face for his company.

Unfortunately, not all customer service is of a positive nature, especially when the provider reacts in a very negative manner. Why? Because they sometimes forget that it is the customer, not the provider, who establishes the rules. When we allow negative emotions or thought processes to direct our actions when dealing with customers, the customer service experience is not very pleasant. Make sure you understand why a person is reacting the way they are reacting. Have you ever approach a friend or acquaintance who was laughing for no apparent reason? How often do you inquire, "What? What's so funny?" When something goes wrong in a business relationship for reasons not apparent to you, you should make this same type of inquiry.

Remember when the "ugly American" was the one who went to foreign countries and embarrassed the rest of us? Now, the ugly Americans have decided, "Why travel?" They are quite content to be ugly right here at home, on the job, in public establishments, and, thanks to the internet, in the not-so-privacy of their own homes. It is the bleed-over effect onto the job that we are most concerned with.

Poor customer service is becoming an accepted norm in our society. Why? As **Larry Winget** said, "People simply don't care. Employees don't care if they do a good job or a bad job. Their bosses don't seem to care one way or another either." This is where the followership gets totally off course. The only way to right the ship is to give them something to care about. That something may be simply reminding them why they took the job in the first place.

> *"Remember, if you want to eat the fruit, you are going to have to go out on a limb sometime."*

Change

If you're not changing, you're done. Holding on to the past or past ways of doing business is a fast track to nowhere in today's business and technology. Much of what you learn in school or college is outdated before you graduate. Flexibility is the key to continued success in today's society.

Dr. Hugh O'Neill of the University of North Carolina's Kenan-Flagler Business School opinioned that what we learn from ages 7 to 17 establishes the pathway of our behavior in later life. These learned behaviors become hardwired in our brains, and the older we get, the more difficult it becomes to change the behavior, and *change* is the operative word in good customer service.

"Men are anxious to improve their circumstances, but are unwilling to improve themselves; they therefore remain bound." Those words of **James Allen**, written centuries ago, are as true today as ever. As a follower, once we allow apathy to become the standard of our work ethic, we are bound to remain in an unchanged station of life. Success is not gained by changing your situation; it is gained by changing you! Self improvement is a must. We must be willing to change ourselves to increase our value; to our customers, our company, and ourselves.

Changing ourselves also includes accepting personal responsibility for all of our actions. The responsible follower adheres to all safety rules to protect themselves as well as their shipmates. They recognize the work place is no place for horseplay, complacency, or ignoring safety standards. One of the greatest quotes I've ever heard is, "Statistics show that 90% of all accidents start with, Hey, watch this!"

> "Personally, I am always willing to learn,
> although I do not always like being taught."
> -Winston Church

Experience Power

There is another important power that followers must embrace to secure their future success: the power of experience. As a follower, there are going to be times, especially when doing something for the first time, when you don't know what you don't know. And the only way you will learn is either by <u>not doing it</u> and being told that you <u>should</u> have, or by doing something that you didn't know that you *shouldn't* be doing. It is absolutely impossible to un-ring a bell. Doing something right the first time is tantamount to prevention of bad habits. It is extremely difficult and time consuming to cure bad habits and practices. Prevention is easier, faster, and more cost effective. Therefore, it is very important that we take every opportunity to learn and know our job. One of my favorite audio books is ***The Slight Edge, by Jeff Olsen***. The author profoundly points out that our highest level of anxiety comes at our lowest level of experience. And it's true, most of us are most nervous the first time we attempt a new, foreign task. Attention to detail, performing the task correctly under supervision with corrective feedback, and confidence in your abilities will be rewarded with success.

Customer Service

International motivational speaker **Willie Jolley** says, "Excellence is still the best job security." Excellence is about not assuming you know what the customer wants; you listen and get the facts, then provide the product or service. Here's a short story I once heard that illustrates what can happen if you assume you know what the customer wants. A young ensign is working late at the Pentagon one evening. As he clocks out of his office at about 8:00 p.m. he sees the Admiral standing by the classified document shedder in the hallway, a piece of paper in his hand.

"Do you know how to work this thing?" the Admiral asks. "My secretary's gone home and I don't know how to run it." "Yes, sir," says the young ensign, who turns on the machine, takes the paper from the Admiral, and feeds it into the machine. "Thanks," says the Admiral, "I just need one copy..."

Customer service can be, and should be, fun. I recall a golf outing several friends and I took to beautiful Southern Pines, North Carolina. Everything was breathtaking, from the road trip to the perfectly manicured fairways we enjoyed. On our second day we played at Southern Pines Golf Club, established in 1906, although you'd hardly know it to look at it.

At the turn (golf talk for going to the number 10 tee box to begin the back nine) there is a food stand run by Mrs. Jane, a wonderfully cheerful senior citizen who I'm sure is very popular throughout the region. It was evident that Mrs. Jane pretty much runs things on the back nine. Adjacent to the food stand is a men's room. In the men's room over the urinal she had placed a hand written sign that read, "Please notify Mrs. Jane of any plumbing problems (ours, not yours)—Mrs. Jane." That is a simple lesson in good customer service, and how you make yourself memorable.

Customer service provides numerous opportunities in followership; some to succeed, and some to fail. Opportunities to improve listening skills, interpersonal communications, coordination of efforts, and organizational skills arise regularly. Followership is the essence and foundation of success because even for the entrepreneur, learning has to take place in order to be successful. The learning required to be successful includes (but is not limited to) listening, interpersonal communications, coordination of efforts, and organizational skills. Do not neglect the importance of followership. This ship is critical to the success and well being of the fleet.

The Read On Followership Summary

My friend Nancy O gave one of the most important lessons on followership I've ever heard, which is "stay in your lane, and know your role." Followers are hired for one reason, and one reason only . . . to fill a need. Once you are on board, you have one of two choices; to become an asset, or a liability. To become an asset, bring something to the table. Having something to give at the right time, i.e., an idea, suggestions outside the box, improving on ideas or processes already in place, that's a lane you want to be in. On the other hand, being a slacker, troublemakers, having regular unexcused absences or tardiness are indicators you don't know your role. Be an asset; try not to miss it by two letters.

CHAPTER 3

Relationship

Three Things Customers Want:

- *They want the best*
- *They want it now*
- *They want it free . . . or on sale*

Of all the lessons in success to learn, this one is critical. The one ship that every business owner strives for is the relationship. Not just any relationship, or a short-term relationship, but lasting, positive relationships. Let's take a look at an outstanding example on relationships through a short quiz. Although the creator of the quiz is unknown, the example it provides is invaluable.

1. Name the five wealthiest people in the world.
2. Name the last five Heisman trophy winners.
3. Name the last five winners of the Miss America contest.
4. Name five people who have won the Nobel or Pulitzer Prize.
5. Name the last five Academy Award winners for best actor and actress.
6. Name the last five World Series winners.

How did you do?

The point is, we do not easily remember the headliners of yesterday. These are no second-rate achievers. They are the best in their fields. But the applause dies. Awards tarnish. Achievements are forgotten. Accolades and certificates are buried with their owners.

Now try a different quiz:

1. Name five teachers who aided your journey through school.
2. Name five friends who have helped you through a difficult time.
3. Name five people who have taught you something worthwhile.
4. Name five people who have made you feel appreciated and special.
5. Name five people you enjoy spending time with.
6. Name five heroes whose stories have inspired you.

Was that easier? The lesson is that the people who make a difference in your life are not the ones with the most credentials, the most money, or the most awards. They are the ones that care about you. Do something today for someone else that will put you on that someone's list of the truly important people in their life. A nugget that I have shared for years is that you may never know whose life you may be touching, but always remember that you may be touching lives.

That's the importance of building and establishing relationships; lasting relationships. Because in business the best customers are repeat customers, and you get repeat customers not just based on price or even product quality. **Julie Langenkamp**, Editor in Chief, DM Review (May 2008), writes about the "Ah Ha" moment. She describes it as, "The intersection of insight and understanding." The "ah ha" moment is most often the one that creates the lasting relationship between you and the customer, and the leader and the follower.

There are warning signs in every relationship when there is a problem. You will note many of these are the same in both personal and professional relationships. Although there are many, some of the most notable are:

- Declining performance
- Delayed deliveries
- Hard to find/hard to talk to
- Not sharing information

- Ignoring
- Failure to acknowledge the relationship

It doesn't take much thought to see how each of these issues can negatively impact the relationship, but it is very important to recognize them.

Success in relationships, especially between leader and follower, carries a level of importance that is hard to put into words and is often overlooked. While attending a business school course at the University of North Carolina, Professor Rick Gilkey expressed it better than any I've ever heard: "Our most valuable asset goes down the elevator and out the door each night, and we hope to God he [or she] comes back the next day." The minute we lose sight of this, we're heading for a shipwreck.

Today's followers are intelligent and sophisticated. They respond to intelligent and sophisticated instructions and directions. Unlike the proud soldiers we send off to defend this great nation who can march until told to stop, or stop until told to march, today's followers need a vision to buy into, a course to set sail for, and a destination that is mutually beneficial to all. Always remember that the followers are the ambassadors of any business; they have the power to make or break the customer relationship. The follower must always be aware that on the relationship, the four most important words in business are, "May-I-help-you?"

The Read On Relationship Summary

The relationship requires complimentary exchanges between parties, and the exchange has to be beneficial to all in order to achieve quality results. William Arthur Ward said, "Do more than belong: participate. Do more than care: help. Do more than believe: practice. Do more than be fair: be kind. Do more than forgive: forget. Do more than dream: work." For any relationship to be successful, everyone needs to participate, and put in the work. If there is one truism, it is that it takes work to make a relationship work.

> "You can easily judge the character of a man
> by how he treats those who can do nothing for him."

Section 1 Review: Chapters 1, 2, and 3

The Read: Leadership, Followership, & Relationship

1. Why is it more important to measure accomplishments than to measure activity?

   _____
   _____
   _____
   _____

2. Name three differences between a leader and a manager.

   _____
   _____
   _____
   _____

3. Why is it important for leaders to be fearless in dealing with followers?

   _____
   _____
   _____
   _____

4. List the 4-Rs and how they relate to followers.

   _____
   _____
   _____
   _____

5. Dr. Hugh O'Neill of the University of North Carolina's Kenan-Flagler Business School opinioned that what we learn from ages 7 to 17 establishes the pathway of our behavior in later life. Explain how this may impact followers?

_____
_____
_____
_____

6. Explain the dynamics of how/why our highest level of anxiety comes at our lowest level of experience.

_____
_____
_____
_____

7. Name the three things that the customer wants.
   1)_____
   2)_____
   3)_____

8. What are the warning signs in a relationship heading for trouble?

_____
_____
_____
_____

9. Why is it important to understand that followers are the ambassadors of your business?

_____
_____
_____
_____

THE NEED

In The Need, again we look at need in its defined form; a requirement, necessary duty, or obligation; a lack of something wanted or deemed necessary; necessity arising from the circumstances of a situation or case. In other words, we look at what is specifically needed to be successful aboard the three ships, i.e., character traits, knowledge, skills, abilities, etc.

CHAPTER 4

Leadership

> *"If Leaders are to build greatness in their units they must inspire trust. Fundamental to inspiring trust are integrity, respect, and loyalty. The need for honesty in the work place cannot be over emphasized. Put simply, people will not follow nor will they make sacrifices for someone they do not trust, and the fastest way to lose trust is through dishonest behavior. Trust is built by leaders who do what is right—for their units, their people and themselves."*
> —*Air University, Air Command and Staff College, "Leadership in Warfare 5510"*

Three lessons needed in leadership that really ring true for me came from a fellow Toastmaster, Distinguished Toastmaster **Aref D**. While delivering one of his many outstanding speeches, Aref emphasized the importance of doing these things:

- surround yourself with positive, not yes people
- seek out positive lessons from each negative situation
- recognize every positive as a blessing

In many ways, leadership is a team sport. Without the team, there is no need for a leader. These three elements, provided primarily from the team, help pave a path of success for a leader. The leader must proactively seek these things out.

The importance in distinguishing the differences between "positive" and "yes" people cannot be overstated. Leaders can be either too close to a situation, or too far removed from it to effect correct course headings or solutions. That is why on the leadership, it is important to have a strong, positive XO (Executive Officer), and not a "yes" man. This was profoundly demonstrated in the movie **Crimson Tide**. The strong willed leader, played by **Gene Hackman**, bought in an equally strong willed XO, played by **Denzel Washington**. Had Washington's character been a "yes" person versus a "positive" person, a catastrophic event (war) would have taken place.

> *"It is better to be making the news than taking the news."*

To seek out positive lessons from each negative situation is a lesson often overlooked in business. Many businesses will take a bad situation and write it off as a cost of doing business. Others get a false sense of security based on recent success and become comfortable with their position. Case in point is a situation that took place within Dell Computers. In his articles **Failure to change can be fatal, even for industry leaders**, columnist **Sidney Hill, Jr.** relates how Dell, an industry leader in personal computers, had failed to move quickly enough beyond their "... direct-to-customer e-commerce sales model," and allowed rival Hewlett-Packard to gain market share on them. Dell sought out the positive lessons. According to Mr. Hill's articles, the company "... introduced a high-end line of PCs and notebooks, the XPS, aimed at PC gamers, and announced plans to open retail stores in New York and Dallas." There is an old adage that those who do not learn from their history are doomed to repeat it. I really like the way William Arthur Ward expressed it when he said, "Failure is delay, but not defeat. It is a temporary detour, not a dead-end street." Success depends upon the strategy you implement. As my friend Larry P says, *strategy* comes before success... even in the dictionary.

And lastly, recognize every positive as a blessing. Why is this important? In business (as in life) it is hard to plan for or capture the intangibles, but very important to recognize and celebrate them. It doesn't take much to make a person feel valued. Actually it takes about the same amount of effort to ignored and make them feel they have no value at all. A public pat on the back, a smile and a "Good morning, Tina" can pay more dividends than you know. There is a lot of uncertainty in business today, and part of that is the uncertainty of knowing if what you are doing is good enough and if it is appreciated. Followers don't want to feel that they are between the dog and the hydrant. As a leader, you can do a lot to ensure they don't feel that way.

> *"Failure is the opportunity to begin again more intelligently."*
> *- Henry Ford*

Levels of Employment

The importance of a leader knowing the crew on the followership is one of the leader's highest priorities. Throughout my working life I have discovered there is a five-stage hierarchy to employment. As a leader, it is essential to recognize which level both existing and potential employees fall into. Doing so will provide you with an acute awareness of expected performance and benefits from individual followers.

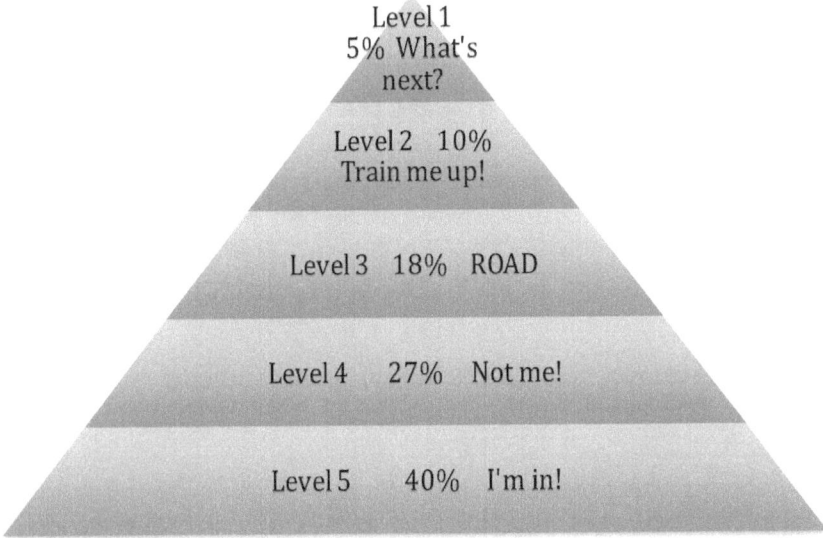

Level 5, "I'm in!" This is the base level, 40-percentile range, where most new followers fall. Their primary objective was to just get in the door, and they made it. This is not necessarily a bad thing, depending on what they bring to the table to contribute to the organization. Many companies consider followers in this level as probationary followers. This time frame, usually 90 days to a year, is where followers must prove themselves.

Level 4, "Not me!" This is the next step up in the hierarchy, and consist of about 27-percent of followers who have successfully passed the probationary period and are now just on board. *Not me* doesn't volunteer for anything, and doesn't want to be called upon for anything either. As my friend Frankie would say, he doesn't want to fish or cut bait; just lie around the deck and eat off of what others bring to the table. The leader must take swift, firm action in dealing with *Not me*, or risk lowering morale among the rest of the crew.

Level 3, "The ROAD." This stems back from my military days, but is absolutely applicable to industry. ROAD is an acronym for *retired on active duty*, and it is easy to recognize these folks. This middle tier of about 18-percent of the workforce is home of some who stop working a little too soon, long before their actual retirement date. Some do because of a misplaced sense on entitlement. Others do because they have slipped through the system as a *"Not me"* to reach the point of retirement. And then there are those few who had made positive contributions to the organization for years, but simply became frustrated with the direction of the company, compensation packages, or even some of their co-workers; old and new. If the leader is really keeping a close eye on his crew, he/she will recognize these ROAD folks, and make necessary course corrections.

Level 2, "Train me up!" This is the leaders joy, that core group of about 10-percent of the workers loaded with lots of potential and eager to learn. They are in it to win and genuinely want to be the best they can be at what they do. The leader's task here is to keep them motivated, gainfully employed, and provide every possible training opportunity, and opportunities to excel. These are the ones who will aspire to the next and final level.

Level 1, "What's next?" The leader's elite few of about 5-percent. You've won their hearts. They're competent, qualified, willing, and ready for whatever comes next. The only problem the leader has here is holding on to his Level 1 crewmembers, because he knows that pretty soon they will command a leadership of their own. Here's a reality check for you. You can employ any number of people, but they will only work for you if/when you win their hearts.

During my tenure with the Department of Defense, I had upwards of 120 people under my supervision at a time. Although the numbers will vary based on the size of the company, you will find more often than not that the percentages of these levels of employment hold true. We use to have an expression that it wasn't the size of the ship that made the sailor sick; it was all that motion going on in the ocean. Keep an eye on the motion going on in your organization's ocean. What's making your people sick?

Leadership Need Summary

The leader needs to maintain an acute awareness of the things his team's members value, individually and collectively. Many years ago Socrates observed that, "There is only one good, knowledge, and one evil, ignorance." There is a need for awareness on the part of the leader. Awareness will help overcome the evil of ignorance.

CHAPTER 5

Followership

> *"The tragedy of life doesn't lie in not reaching your goal. The tragedy lies in having no goal to reach. It isn't a calamity to die with dreams unfulfilled, but it is a calamity not to dream.... It is not a disgrace not to reach the stars, but it is a disgrace to have no stars to reach for. Not failure, but low aim is sin."*
> —Benjamin Elijah Mays

I once heard that the ten most powerful two-letter words in the English language are, *"If it is to be, it is up to me."* No truer words were ever spoken. Each of us is responsible for our own success. Sure, leadership is responsible for providing the cargo of such things as training, tools and equipment, upward mobility, etc. But it is the follower's responsibility to take advantage of training opportunities, learn to properly and expertly use the tools and equipment provided, and look to move up or jump ship in the organization—from followership to leadership. Attitude, more than aptitude, is what most propels you forward.

> *"A bad attitude is like a flat tire-*
> *You can't get very far until you change it."*

I'm In

So you've reached Level 5 on the Employment Pyramid, you're in. In your personal inventory, think about this. In the work that you do, do you think you are important or not? Are you as important behind the counter as that supervisor in the office across the hall? Do you think you are better than your current position and should have been picked for something better? Do you find being a "deck hand" an insignificant challenge? After all, you're just a small fish in a big ocean, right? And your current situation is not your final destination, so why expend more effort than necessary? Many people struggle to find their purpose in life. Maybe that's because they don't know where to look. I suggest looking in three areas; dreams, potential, and power! Why here?

Because as you go forward in life, these three elements, more than anything else, will shape your future and chart your life course. Looking at each one closely, dreams are sequence, sounds and feelings experienced while sleeping. The mental image you develop of your future is created primarily by the dreams you have, and the actions you take to realize your dreams. Potential means existing in possibility: capable of development into actuality. This is the point in life where you must honestly determine, "Is it in me." This is important because sometimes we get a mismatch. Think about it. Some things we are gifted to do, but don't particularly like doing. On the other hand, some things we really enjoy doing, but are not really gifted to do. We can all point to people we know that fit into one of these categories. A quick look at the early season episodes of American Idol proves this—many of the contestants really enjoy trying to sing, but certainly are not gifted at it. And then there is power. Power is a measure of a person's ability to control the environment around them, including the behavior of other people. Notice it doesn't say anything about the person's position, just the measure of their ability. Does a two-year old screaming at the top of her lungs in a crowded restaurant have power in that environment? Is she influencing the behavior of other people in that restaurant? Absolutely! She has power.

And so do you. From your position behind the counter, you have the power to make or break customer relationships for your company. You are a person of influence. Your current situation does not have to be your final destination, but if you are to realize your dreams, you must develop the habit of doing your best . . . from whatever position you hold. This is what I call hustling while you wait; waiting to develop your potential, for your opportunity, for your shot at realizing your dream. In the math of life, sometimes it takes 3 (dreams, potential, and power) . . . to get to 1 (your purpose). You are absolutely important, and what you do absolutely matters, so do your best.

> *There are two primary choices in life: accept conditions as they are or accept the responsibility for changing them.*
> —Dick Friesz

Eligible

Success on the followership or the leadership requires both a purpose and a plan. These two must work in concert with each other, and they have to be developed early in one's working life. The plan has to identify the desired career path, and it must include purposeful preparation, to include education and training, personal development, and both short term and long term goals.

Before you can be successful in any business venture the first thing you have to be is eligible. Merriam-Webster defines eligible as fit or proper to be chosen; worthy of choice; desirable. I'm sitting in church on Sunday morning and my Bishop has directed this message on eligibility to the youth. While listening to him I'm thinking how much this applies to any and everyone entering the workforce.

Now, being a guy and into sports, the first association I thought of in terms of being eligible was with high school sports. In order to be eligible, student athletes must go to class, maintain a certain grade point average, complete all mandatory class work assignments, and refrain from getting into trouble either on campus or off (i.e., fighting, gang related activities, etc.).

There are so many positive steps one can take to make themselves eligible for prospective employers. Positive attitude, pleasant personality, training and formal education, personal hygiene, and dress and appearance all come readily to mind. Most of these, in the mind of prospective employers, are expectations. Once your resume has been reviewed and you are referred for an interview, you are expected to dress professionally, be pleasant, and have a level of training and education to show that you are capable of meeting the requirements of the job; you are eligible.

However, eligible is one side of a coin. The other side is being ineligible. Merriam-Webster defines ineligible as not qualified for an office or position. A quick look at just some of the things that renders one ineligible in the workplace today includes lack of training and/or formal education, poor hygiene and personal appearance, too many or offensive tattoos, especially exposed ones, and (the most important in my mind) a poor or indifferent attitude. Your name can be a source of ineligibility. Other factors include faddish hairstyles, and a major hurdle in today's society, obesity.

The plan and the purpose are major determinants in future success and accomplishments. Many students planned to go to college, and do, but they have no purpose beyond getting a formal education. Others say their purpose is to become politician, lawyer, teacher, rapper, professional baller, whatever, but have no plan for putting in the work to get there. A plan and a purpose; one without the other is not effective. Together, not only do they make you eligible . . . they can make you unstoppable.

Driven

What drives you? Are you driven to succeed, or do you operate from the "carrot and stick" approach? Many people have an expectancy theory, expecting to have fortune come their way because they feel the world owes them something. I heard some place that the world owes you nothing; it was here first. Rare is the individual with the drive to stay the course and do the right thing on a daily basis.

Drive doesn't come overnight. It is a character trait developed over years, urged on by a desire to have something that really means something to you. What that *something* is varies from one individual to the next, a big house, fancy car, corner office job, status, whatever the drive is. How hard you pursue the dream depends on how big your drive is . . . your will.

Sad to say, but many followers operate from the carrot and stick approach to employment. This is especially true once they reach Level 3 on the Employment Pyramid and go ROAD. The carrot and stick policy is one of offering rewards and punishments as inducements to obtain desired behaviors. This is both labor and time intensive for the leader, and production is based on increased rewards or increased punishments, neither of which can be sustained productively for very long.

Drive is often circumvented due to necessity, i.e., lack of funds to get the necessary education or training, non-availability of required training, or sometimes simply not knowing what you don't know. Professional speaker Bill Gove spoke on "The Positive Power of Doing." In this, he said, "Life is not lived at the level of "I'll think about it" or "I'll do it when I feel like it." Life is about doing what is in front of you, and doing it now, whether you feel like it or not."

That's what it means to be driven. The ability to reach deep inside yourself, especially during those times when you don't feel like it, and doing what needs to be done. Do you have the drive? Is it in you?

The Most Important Thing

As a follower, what do you think is the most important of these four traits in your working life, *knowledge, skill, understanding*, or *will*? To be fair, let me explain them a little first. I don't think it will take very long for you to see where I'm going and then make your decision.

Knowledge is simply awareness or familiarity gained from experience. The more things we are exposed to that we can obtain facts and intelligence from, the greater our base of knowledge. Skill, on the other hand, is our level of expertise based on talent and (especially) practice. Understanding speaks to an individual's perception or judgment of a situation (which in my mind relates back to knowledge). And finally, there is will. The definition I find most appropriate is *energy of intention*.

Although each of these qualities are important to the follower, I am convinced that will is the most important. Knowledge is great, but knowledge can be gained actively (actually getting out and experiencing things) or passively (sitting at home watching TV or reading). Skill is a tremendous asset, but often comes too easy for some and is not recognized as valuable. If you think for just a few moments, I'm sure you can think of someone you know working in a job they are not happy with, but are exceptional cooks, painters, artist, etc. Not recognizing the demand for their skill, or (most probably) fear is keeping them from capitalizing on a skill set.

Understanding probably takes the most time and energy in dealing with a problem. It requires you to take in all available information, patiently break it down, view it from many different angles, and then make decisions.

Will is a personal challenge on your integrity. What are you willing to do? How much effort are you willing to expand? Do you always give your very best? When and where do you draw the line between what is good, and what is good enough?

If you ask most leaders which of these qualities they list as most desired, I'm pretty sure they will list *will* at the top. Why? None of the other three are indicative that a follower will advance much further than Level 4 on the hierarchy. There are knowledgeable sloths in organizations all around the country. Likewise, there are mismatched skill sets throughout organizations (the young man working in a small, cramped office repairing computer components has outstanding people skills and should be out front representing your company). Understanding alone is not sufficient. Far too many organizations have individuals who understand problems within the company, knew a proposal was not going to work and had a positive solution, but never said a word (either Level 4 or Level 3 people).

But the people with the will, the ones who will stand up and make a difference; who are not afraid of failure or the possibility of ridicule, these are the folks of true value. Will, not skill, will get you up the hill. Knowledge can be gained, skill can be attained, understanding will come with exposure and experience. However, if a person is willing, all three of the other traits can be acquired to help on the assent to Level 1 employment.

Worth

One of the greatest weaknesses on the followership is lack of awareness of self worth. It is extremely difficult to develop a goal that is worthy of you, if you don't know what you're worth. I know people who apply for jobs, go on interviews, and do a great job until the question, "What salary range are you looking for?" comes up. They are totally lost! No idea of their self worth.

We all have two jobs that we are responsible for unto ourselves; an *outside* job and an *inside* job. Our outside job requires us to step outside of ourselves and examine our ship's location (where am I, where was I supposed to be, am I on course or off course?). Our inside job requires us to take an internal audit of our knowledge, skills, and abilities (where am I strong, where am I lacking?) and establish strategic, short-range goals to shore up weak areas.

Take an inventory of yourself; strengths, weaknesses, growth potential. How much education do you have, and in what areas? What are your professional skills and life skills? What are you prepared to do to achieve your goals? Know what you're worth. And once you know, go out with the expectation of getting what you're worth.

My friend Lou talks of the importance of being prepared to live life in 3D. He often teaches that life will throw up roadblocks of deception, distractions, and destruction. Deception in the form of people not dealing honestly and truthfully with you. Distractions from your goals by other people (family and friends, too), things (i.e., recreational activities versus focusing on goals) are almost certain to occur. And, the destruction of dreams, relationships, and opportunities, from both internal and external factors.

And it doesn't stop there. Followers must take the initiative for self-development. In this age of instant information, rapidly changing technology, and a highly intelligent customer base, continuing education is a must. Followers must possess both tacit knowledge (understood without being openly expressed) and explicit knowledge (fully and clearly expressed or demonstrated—leaving nothing merely implied) of the product or service being provided. This is a "do-or-die" age of business we live in, and Darwin's evolutionary theory is alive and well. Self-development opportunities abound in community college courses, seminars, webinars, and on-line university courses, just to name a few. Your self-development does have a cost associated with it, but if you look at the opportunity cost of failing to develop your talents to keep pace in the market place, it is almost assured your ship will not come in.

Followership Need Summary

Today's business challenges don't just require followership, it requires good followership. The job market is very competitive and the talent pool is more educated and sophisticated than ever. It takes dedication and work to prepare one's self to become eligible and attractive to prospective employers. Having a plan and a purpose will help you identify what you need to do to improve your eligibility. Long ago Henry Adams said, "They know enough who know how to learn." As my father use to say, ain't that the truth?

CHAPTER 6

Relationship

"Between stimulus and response, there is a space. In that space is our power to choose our response. In our response lies our growth and our freedom."
—Stephen Covey

Every relationship carries with it an implied responsibility by both the supplier and the receiver. A quick definition of responsibility is duty; obligation. If you are charged with or accept a task, then you have a duty or obligation to fulfill that task. There are many excuses for failing to accept personal responsibility in a relationship, and most of them are found in the blame game. There always seems to be something or someone else to blame for why we didn't live up to our responsibilities. The bottom line, however, is if you have the ability, and you fail in your response, the blame is yours.

Think! Think long and hard before entering into a relationship and obligating yourself. Be sure the relationship is a good fit. Look it over from every possible angle. Internationally renowned author and speaker Dr. Wayne Dyer said, "When you change the way you look at things, the things you look at change."

Let me share another story with you from my friend Sandy. He said, "One of my bosses told me something one day that I have never forgotten. It is said that it takes months and sometimes years for a company to obtain a steady customer (one who comes back to you), and it takes about fifteen seconds to lose one. All you have to do is treat a customer like he (or she) is not a customer. I will give you an example. The wife and I were in a Burger

_____ restaurant early one morning, about a year ago (last time). It was an early fall day and the doors were open. My wife was chilly so I walked over and shut the door. The manager of the store jumped over the counter and re-opened the door. He never once said anything to me. It made me feel as if I had done something terribly wrong. We immediately left. I have not been in a Burger ____ since. You say that was just an incident; that it was one misunderstanding between me and a manager at one of many Burger ____'s. Yes you could be right, I suppose."

The point to Sandy's story is, it only takes once! One moment of inconsiderate, poor judgment and a relationship is broken. The question you have to ask yourself is, "Do I have so many customers that I can afford to lose any?"

Life in 3-D

Let's go back to Lou's story for a minute. The most destructive life style in business is living and dealing in 3D; deception, distractions, and destruction. Deception is the act of convincing another to believe information that is not true, or not the whole truth as in certain types of half-truths. Many businesses deceive their customers by making promises they know they cannot deliver on. These customers, in turn, violate their integrity because they have made commitments to *their* customers based on delivery of goods or services promised by you. This cycle of deception creates a vortex that drags the relationship under and can lead to an abandoned ship (business).

Distractions are that which distracts, divides the attention, or prevents concentration. Distractions occur when we allow ourselves to be diverted from our obligations and miss deadlines self-imposed or made freely to customers. For example, a graphic artist I contracted a job out to begin in earnest working on my project. Before he could complete my work, he received a huge contract for work with a large business firm in the DC area. Because of the size and scope of this new contract, my delivery date was delayed (read that "ignored") in favor of the new business. In this case, I guess size really did matter. Remember, trust is the basis of all relationships. Once you violate your integrity, the relationship is on a crash course with the rocks of ruin.

Destruction can take many forms, and can be internal or external. One important form of destruction that is often overlooked is destructive dependencies. Professional dependencies on services being provided through business relationship are one example. We can become dependent on others to a point that it leads to our destruction. Take the situation above with my graphic artist. If you allow yourself to become so locked in to a source, from misguided loyalty or whatever, you can be headed for destruction. However, destructive dependencies can also be of a personal nature, i.e., alcohol, narcotics, gambling, inappropriate sexual relationship, etc. Sometimes, what you conceal is far more important than what you reveal. Any of these destructive dependencies can place the relationship on a crash course with failure.

Relationship Components

Although I'm sure there are probably many more and different ones, let's look at the different components of a successful relationship. The components I feel are most important are:

- character
- competency
- results

For those on board the relationship, character speaks to the personal side of the equation. In dealings with customers, followers, and business partners, character refers to the establishment of trust, communications skills (both listening and speaking), acceptance of responsibilities, and establishing positive associations. Character, notable or conspicuous traits, is what defines an individual. **Donald Trump's** character defines him as being driven to the heights of success in the real estate business. **Tiger Wood's** character is defined in both his physical fitness and his mental toughness. Ask yourself, what character traits do you exhibit that define you?

While we're discussing character, let me personalize this a little further. If you know or discern that you really have a strong dislike for your job, begin immediately searching for employment elsewhere. If you find that you cannot maintain a positive attitude and do the job in a professional manner, quit. Don't allow customers, co-workers, or the company to suffer because you can't or refuse to give your best effort. In other words, when you lose your desire to do the job, don't lose your integrity, too. No other trait more visibly defines your character like your integrity.

Competency refers to the knowledge, skills, ability and mental discipline one possesses in doing his or her job. Listening, learning new skills, reading to keep abreast of new developments in your profession, being patient in dealing with others, transitioning in changing environments, and coming up with new, creative problem-solving techniques all enhance and develop competency. Competency equates to excellence, and excellence equates to how well you use your knowledge, skills and abilities. However, without the mental discipline to get in there and do what is expected of you and what you know needs doing, whether someone is looking or not, requires a special brand of intestinal fortitude, aka, guts. As D.A. Benton said, "Guts are a combination of confidence, courage, conviction, strength of character, stick-to-itiveness, pugnaciousness, backbone, and intestinal fortitude." It may be time to take inventory of yourself to see what you've got.

Author Napoleon Hill stated, "Millions of people falsely believe that knowledge is power. It is nothing of the sort! It is only *potential* power. It becomes power only when it is organized into definite plans of action and directed to a definite end. It is not what you know—but what you do, with what you know." It is only when you maximize your potential that you become competent.

Both your character and your competency are very important, but as I stated earlier, ultimately it is only the results that matter. Customers, shareholders, banks and bosses care very little for the "how;" that's the leader's problem. Customers, shareholders, banks and bosses are only concerned (for the most part) with the results; the bottom line. Are you getting results? Are you making progress? There's an old Navy saying that when you're making slow or little progress, you're dragging the anchor.

Give Them What They Want

Business, when viewed in its purest form, is a simple, relationship process. Relationships are based on wants, and the word "want" has two definitions for our business purposes; either the desire for something, or the lack of something. My friend **Bob Yates**, founder and CEO of *Circle of Champions*, explained that there are three very simple steps to a business relationship:

- find out what "they" (customers) want (desire for) in the market place
- go get it
- give it to them

That's it! Pure and simple. First, find out what they want. How do you do that? It's a relationship . . . *go talk to them and ask!* And once you're sure you know what they want (and you really need to be sure), *go get it (lack of)*. Once you get it, verify that it is indeed what they want, in the right quantity, at the right time, and go *give it to them*. Of course there will be numerous course corrections as you chart your ships on the voyage to success (changes in "wants" in the market place, how to make, innovate, acquire what "they" want, and giving it to them via such methods as direct sales, internet, TV infomercial sales, etc.). But at least you know the destination . . . a positive, lasting relationship.

The bottom line is, relationships always go back to choices and consequences. How you present, associate, and negotiate with people will determine just how successful you will be; in business and in life. I recall a rhyme from years ago that is often used today as a reminder of how the little things in life can have major impacts on a relationship. In fact, it was such a powerful reminder, Benjamin Franklin used it in his Poor Richard's Almanac in the 1700s. His version reads:

> *For want of a nail a shoe was lost.*
> *For want of a shoe a horse was lost.*
> *For want of a horse the rider was lost.*
> *For want of a rider the battle was lost.*
> *For want of a battle the kingdom was lost.*
> *All for the want of a horseshoe nail.*

What small things have you lost? In your business, and your personal life? And all for want of . . . what?

Relationships Need Summary

The key need in all relationships is the need for reciprocity. There must be clear, reciprocal benefits to all parties involved if the relationship is to be, and is to remain, successful. The question on everyone's favorite radio station, WII-FM (What's-In-It-For-Me) must be answered, and regularly reinforced. People want to feel like they are wanted, and need to feel like they are needed. Understanding and relating to those feelings ensures smooth sailing on the relationship.

Section 2 Review: Chapters 4, 5, and 6

The Need: Leadership, Followership, & Relationship

1. Distinguish the differences between *positive* and *yes* people.

2. As relates to the Levels of Employment hierarchy, what is Level 3 and explain why it can be detrimental to an organization.

3. Identify the ten most powerful two-letter words in the English language and their impact on followership.

4. Name at least three steps a follower can take to make himself eligible, and three steps that makes him ineligible.

4. Of the four important traits in working life, *knowledge, skill, understanding,* or *will,* which do you think is the most important and why?

5. Dr. Wayne Dyer said, "When you change the way you look at things, the things you look at change." What does this mean to you?

   _____
   _____
   _____
   _____

6. On the relationship, what does the word character speak to?

   _____
   _____
   _____
   _____

7. Explain the dynamics of the three simple steps to a business relationship and their impact on an organization.

   _____
   _____
   _____
   _____

THE SEED

Although the dictionary defines seed to mean "the fertilized, matured ovule of a flowering plant, containing an embryo or rudimentary plant; any propagative part of a plant, including tubers, bulbs, etc., esp. as preserved for growing a new crop; offspring," we look at a slightly different connotation of the word. For our purposes, the seeds we discuss are thought seeds, and we look at the impact of all our <u>thought</u> seeds that produce positive and negative outcomes on the three ships. In a nutshell, "thoughts become things".

CHAPTER 7

Leadership

"The best leadership tool is candor. Candor generates meaning and clears up clutter."
—Rick Grandinetti, Founder & CEO,
Vision Planning, Inc.

Precious Cargo

The precious cargo on all three ships is seeds. Yes seeds, necessary for sustainment in all areas of success. In his book, **As A Man Thinketh**, author **James Allen** compares the human mind to a garden. As with any garden, it will yield based on the seeds planted there; good seed, good fruit. Bad seed, bad fruit.

Every organization is like a garden. The leader is the gardener, and the people are the plants. As with most gardens, many leaders want to go from seed to harvest; it doesn't work that way. Every garden is going to have weeds. You must continuously cultivate before you reap the harvest. Why do leaders try to avoid this step? Because it requires both work and confrontation. Confrontation is a major issue for many leaders. In his daily column for **The Federal Report**, **Mike Causey** wrote (on July 8, 2011), "Some managers are afraid to deal with their "problem kids;" afraid of being fired, sued, or personally attacked. It's not a 'management' problem, it is a leadership problem. The English language is complicated and nuanced in many ways. I see the word manager and I am reminded that managing can also be construed as hanging on, 'coping' as it were."

The leader must cultivate his followers; pull the weeds from the good crop before the life is choked out of them. And don't be surprised to find a snake in the garden from time to time. This is where the confrontation comes in, and in today's society, people try to avoid confrontation as much as possible. But as a leader, it comes with the territory. Expect the occasional snake and prepare for him. Remember, there was even one in the Garden of Eden.

Shoot the Gap

Leadership is primarily about communication. A leader can't be too busy to lead. It is a tremendous mistake for a leader to assume that followers know their jobs, get disappointed with results, but don't want followers to take matters into their own hands. This sends a mixed message. Leaders must take the time to lead, and they must lead through effective communications. To be effective in communications, leaders must first acknowledge and identify the gap in communications between themselves and their followers.

One of the essential activities a leader can perform, or have performed, is a gap analysis. A gap analysis is a tool that identifies not just what resources you have, but more importantly what is missing or needed for your organization to maximize its performance potential. The gap is what leaders are looking for in their budget/fiscal analysis, systems analysis, staffing analysis, personal property and (sometimes) real property analysis. How big is the gap from your best follower to your weakest? From your technology to your competitors? Even if you don't have resources to immediately fill identified gaps, it is still important for the leader to identify and acknowledge them. Why? To realize your service limitations and to plan and project for future actions. As a leader, to get followers to give you what you want, help them get what it is they want. In other words, if you want to inspire people, help people. Leaders must figure ways to stop dragging their anchors and heave them back into the ship to sail on. Shoot the gap, then fill the gap.

> *"Not all questions are seeking an answer . . . some are seeking a reaction. Not everyone who talks to you wants conversation . . . some just want an audience."*

Get it Going On

Larry Wilson of the Wilson Learning Corporation said, "Leadership is not a designated position; it is a phenomenon. It is people following people because they want to, not because they have to." This phenomenon is critical to one's ability to be charged with the precious cargo—the seeds.

I recently found myself on a business trip to Gulfport, Mississippi during Fat Tuesday, also known as Mardi Gras. During my week's stay there, I had breakfast each morning at the same Waffle House. There was an outstanding service provider (I don't like the term "waitress") name Teresa that epitomized the phenomenon described above. Even though there was a manager on duty, everyone on staff, and most of the customers, recognized the true leadership power that Teresa wielded. As my daughter often says, when you got it going on, other people know that you've got it going on.

Setting Standards

Warren Buffet, reportedly the second richest man in the world, is said to write only one letter per year to the CEOs of his companies. In this one letter, he lays out their goals for the year; his seeds. That's it! No staff meetings, no regular calls, just one annual letter. Based on his level of success, it is clear that he places a great deal of importance on assigning the right people to the right job.

You have to set the standards but the followers have to believe in you! You must know your stuff. One of the more powerful lessons in leadership ever taught to me was this simple phrase: "You can't teach, what you don't know and you can't lead where you won't go." So know your stuff, and show your stuff. Somewhere along my travels, I recall hearing that, as a leader, you're in the proving business. The leader's job is to prove that he/she can lead their team to success, and then go out and do it.

Recognizing talent and skill sets, and matching them to the right job is a leadership trait that leads directly to success. It also leads to job satisfaction on the part of the follower. Again, good seed, good fruit. Bad seed, bad fruit.

On the leadership, candor is a great seed to have. When sharing the vision, leaders need to be clear and direct. Their message needs to be congruent in both their verbal and their non-verbal delivery. Keep in mind that people tend to say things they don't really mean to at times, even when they don't open their mouths. How? Through their non-verbals. Remember, by many estimates, over 70% of all communication is non-verbal. Let's look at the seed cargo on the leadership:

1. **Seeds of results**
    - Giving the people what they want, when they want it, how they want it
    - Failing any of the above, make it right; don't make excuses

2. **Seeds of trust**
    - Public trust for customers
    - Corporate trust for employees and business partners

3. **Seeds of expectancy**
    - Quality product for customers
    - Fair and honest dealings with customers, employees and business partners

4. **Seeds of continuous improvement**
    - Always seeking new and better ways to serve the customer
    - Taking every opportunity in a changing market place to find out what the people want. Note that opportunity is not always going to be easy to recognize. It can be right there in front of you and you won't be able to see it (but someone else will and they will capitalized on it). Not only do you have to be looking for opportunity, you have to be ready for it.

5. **Seeds of communication**
    - Always making time not to just hear, but to listen to customers
    - Ensuring you establish role clarity and transparency so people truly know <u>you</u> and what you are about

6. **Seeds of information**
    - Staying abreast of changing technologies and successful business practices
    - Knowledge of what your employees' training and equipment needs are

7. **Seeds of availability**
    - Being both visible and available to speak with customers and employees
    - Recognizing that it is velocity, the ability to move things faster, which will ensure growth and success in business.

Not So Fast

Now, having said all of that about the expectation of the leader, keep in mind that the leader is human and must have a personal life. Far too many get to the top and think the ship can't stay afloat without their hand constantly at the helm. Their days are so packed they run into each other like one long, endless day. Many live by their blackberry (aka "crackberry," because they are hooked) and their calendar. They can find the time to schedule their headaches but can't seem to find time for fun, family, and friends.

In one of my favorite books, *Dr. Stephen R. Covey* in laying out his *7-Habits of Highly Effective People* captured the importance of making time for one's self. In the last habit, Habit 7: Sharpen the Saw, he details how and why self-rejuvenation is good for you and required for good mental health. Habit 7 advises to, "Balance and renew your resources, energy, and health to create a sustainable, long-term, effective lifestyle." Get some exercise, read a good book, go to a game or a play, revisit your spiritual faith, or cross something off of your bucket list. You may be amazed at how you can return to work with a fresh perspective after a little well deserved break, and your followers will probably recognize and appreciate it, too.

Leaderships Seeds Summary

The seeds of leadership are numerous, and vary greatly. Although the leader doesn't plant the seeds for his followers, the task of cultivating the followers falls squarely on the shoulders of the leader. From their attitudes to aptitudes, their vicissitudes to their ineptitude, followers will test the mettle of their leaders, and leaders must be ever prepared for these test. To be prepared, the leader must pull back, step away from time to time, and get perspective. Our most powerful resource is a positive mind. Keep in mind that negative self-talk sets limits on your life. Why? Because you believe what you say about you, more than what anyone else will ever say about you. (I'm sure I've heard that somewhere before.) Be candid, be firm, stay positive, and lead.

CHAPTER 8

Followership

> *"I long to accomplish a great and noble task, but it is my chief duty to accomplish small tasks, as if they were great and noble."*
>
> —Helen Keller

Vision and Creativity

It is the job of leadership to share the vision. It is the expectation of followership to create the means and the atmosphere for personal development, as well as meeting mission requirements. Therefore, the seed to be planted here is the seed of creativity. Remember back to your childhood for a moment. Remember those days when a thought, sight, or sound could send your mind off to a place where everything was clearer, and the impossible seemed very possible? Typically, there were two types of people who interrupted those moments; those who genuinely wanted to know what you were thinking, or those who chastised you to, "Stop day-dreaming and get back to work!"

Forget about the dream stealers for a moment and remember those good dreams. This is one of the greatest losses in America today . . . creativity. We have lost our capacity to dream and create. We all have to accept the fact that not everyone is going to believe in our dreams, and that's okay. Just realize that it is through creativity that fortunes undreamed of are earned. As Nassim Nicholas Taleb points out in his exceptional book *The Black Swan: The Impact of the Highly Improbable*, ". . . no one knew whether a book by a mother on welfare about a boy magician with an odd birthmark would flop or make the author a billionaire." Or, as I like to say, there's only one thing you ever really know, that is that you never really know.

Remember, there are two jobs that we all must step up and take on, an outside job and an inside job. The outside job requires that you step outside of yourself and examine your life; where you are, where you had hoped to be, and what happened. The inside job requires you to take an internal audit of your knowledge, skills and abilities. You have to know where you're strong, know what is lacking, and establish strategies and short-range goals to get you there. In the words of that great American philosopher . . . Yogi Berra, "If you don't know where you are going, you will wind up somewhere else." Now that's creativity.

Attitude

Ever notice how some folks, after they've been on the job for a while, seem to forget why they took the job in the first place? They-needed-a-paycheck! That's why they went looking for employment. That's why they applied, got all dressed up and went in for the interview. They-needed-a-job. Somewhere, over time, they lost sight of that fact. They began to feel their employer owed them something more than "just" a paycheck. What? There use to be a popular expression not too long ago: Don't get it twisted. What you want and what the job owes you may be (and probably are) two entirely different things. The company owes you a paycheck; you owe the company an honest day's work. If you're looking for something beyond that, you may want to consider becoming an entrepreneur. For sure, one of the greatest powers we all possess is our attitude. Irvin Berlin said, "Our attitudes control our lives. Attitudes are a secret power working twenty-four hours a day, for good or bad. It is of paramount importance that we know how to harness and control this great force." You can go a long way on attitude alone. Whether that long way is up or down, depends on your attitude. Check your attitude.

> *"What you do may be more important than what I do, but that doesn't mean that you are more important than me."*

Creativity is about attitude. Top motivational speaker and author Keith Harold said, "Attitude determines whether you are on your way, or in the way." Sometimes, because we lack creativity, we can't seem to get out of our own way. Lack of creativity can lead not only to frustration, but also to depression.

Creativity is fun. Lack of creativity is predictable and, let's face it, boring. For example, I remember hearing a story about this group of college students that got three goats secretly onto campus. They spray painted the numbers 1, 2, and 4 on the side of the goats, and set them free on campus. Campus security rounded up goats 1, 2, and 4 in relatively short order, but no one is really sure how much time was spent looking for goat number 3! Now, who do you think was having fun, and who was being predictable?

Your future depends upon your dreams, but you can't just dream forever. In order to have a dream come true, the first thing you have to do is W-A-K-E U-P! Wake up, and set a course to prepare yourself to realize your dream. Prepare through education, training, and recognizing and taking advantage of opportunities as they present themselves. Albert Einstein said, "Don't let what you cannot do interfere with what you can do." You can prepare.

One of the greatest assets on the followership is creativity. For many of us, we have been blindly led to membership in the greatest nation in the world; *procrasti*nation. Maybe it's time to jump ship and join the most productive nation in the world; *imagi*nation.

The seeds cargo carried on the followership differ from those on the leadership and, when planted in fertile soil, yield a different fruit:

1. Seeds of results
- Recognizing and accepting your role in the business relationship
- Not only knowing, but doing, what it takes to be successful

2. Seeds of trust
- Living up to the trust placed in you by the leader
- Understanding how trust plays a huge role in increasing speed and keeping cost low

3. Seeds of expectancy
- Knowing what is expected of you from customers and leaders

- Fair and honest dealings with customers, employers and business associates

4. **Seeds of continuous improvement**
    - Always seeking new opportunities to increase your value to the company
    - Taking every opportunity in a changing work market to meet and exceed expectations

5. **Seeds of communication**
    - Understanding that on the followership, communications work best when you listen twice as much as you speak
    - Ensuring you communicate your needs as well as your desires up the chain to avoid misunderstandings or feelings of being slighted

6. **Seeds of information**
    - Staying abreast of changing technologies, products, and successful business practices
    - Knowledge of and skill in using new equipment, policies and procedures

7. **Seeds of availability**
    - Being both visible and available when you are suppose to and where you are supposed to be
    - Recognizing the importance of *knowing* your worth, and *showing* your worth, to get *what* you are worth

Bottom line message to send to leaders, make your followers feel welcome, important, and valued.

Followership Seeds Summary

Never lose track of why you took your job in the first place. If that need has been satisfied, then maybe it is time to plant your seed someplace else. However, before you do, recognize that there is a huge advantage to a graceful exit; you always want to keep your options open. If your future plans don't work out, you always want the possibility of being considered for rehire. Always, always, always invest in yourself. The largest room in the world is the room for improvement. There can always be a better you.

CHAPTER 9

Relationship

"Many people are busier <u>protecting</u> their job than <u>doing</u> their job. It's tough being successful in this type of work environment."

Fun

Enjoying your job works hand-in-hand with doing your job. It is important in the development and maintenance of a relationship to invoke humor and levity where situations may be tense of stressful. Let me site another example from my favorite airline, Southwest. Recently, while returning from a business trip in Denver, we were on a flight that was completely booked. During boarding tempers were getting short as passengers were attempting to locate overhead space for their carry-ons, and spending a little too much time in the aisles. This was the statement made by the flight attendant over the public address system: "Good afternoon ladies and gentlemen and welcome aboard Flight 467 to Baltimore. Please find a seat as quickly as possible and store your carry-on bags. This is our last flight and this crew is ready to go home, so let's get this flight under way. Yes, it is totally about us." The laughter could be heard all over the plane as passengers did as they were requested.

Let me sow another relationship seed here. In looking at the relationships between the sexes, I recall reading, "Women marry because they believe <u>he</u> will change one day. Men marry because they believe <u>she</u> will never change. Both are mistaken!" This same thought process can be applied to the business relationship. Customers buy into our business because they believe we will change (one day) with the times. Businesses take their customers for granted because they believe they will never change. You need only to look at our current automotive industry to realize both are mistaken!

The Battle

There is a story of an old Cherokee Indian who was speaking to his grandson. "A fight is going on inside me," he said to the boy. "It is a terrible fight and it is between two wolves. One is evil—he is anger, envy, sorrow, regret, greed, arrogance, self-pity, guilt, resentment, inferiority, lies, false pride, superiority, and ego. The other is good—he is joy, peace, love, hope, serenity, humility, kindness, benevolence, empathy, generosity, truth, compassion, and faith. This same fight is going on inside of you, and inside every person, too." The grandson thought about it for a long minute, and then asked his grandfather, "Which wolf will win?" The old Cherokee replied simply, "The one you feed."

In today's business relationships, there are battles taking place every day, also between two wolves. One is confidence—self-assured, knowledgeable, skillful, competent, attentive, and willing. The other is fear—worried about market conditions, current employment, future status, anxiety, and regret. Which one will win? Depends to a great extent on the customer service experience. Leaders and followers must be aware of the battle being waged inside their customer each time they interact with them.

I heard once that if you are not living on the edge, you're taking up too much space. Don't allow fear to stop you from getting out there and taking chances. Fear will rule you, if you allow it to. Confidence and fear, which one will win? As the old chief said, the one you feed.

Relationship Cargo

What kind of cargo are you carrying on the relationship? From time to time, we all have to lighten our loads, throw some unneeded cargo overboard. Anger, jealousy, envy, and negativity are just some of the expendables that come to mind. What we have to do is recognize both the position and condition we are in, and that will determine the expendable cargo.

Anger, uncontrolled, can be very destructive cargo on the relationship. The book of Proverbs states, "A fool gives full vent to his anger, but a wise man keeps himself under control." Just from observing children, I have always found there to be a very simple definition for anger: I-didn't-get-my-way. Folks who don't get their way tend to get angry, and the more actual or perceived power they have, the greater the degree they tend to vent their anger. This cargo should be marked with a "Highly Explosive" warning label, and identified as one of the first to be cast overboard in rough waters.

Jealousy, those negative thoughts or feelings bought on by insecurity, fear, and anxiety over an anticipated loss of something, is best explained by one simple statement; "Someone else is getting the attention and praise that I deserve." This is more dangerous cargo because it takes the focus off of what you should be doing and puts it on criticizing what others are doing, and why it should be your job because you can do it so much better. Anything that takes your attention and efforts away from your primary task is counter-productive. Jealousy is counter-productive. Get it off of the ship.

Envy is a first cousin to jealousy, and the two terms are often used interchangeably. Aristotle defined envy as, "the pain caused by the good fortune of others." In today's society, it is called "hating," and it is happening every day. People are hating on others for their promotions, good job assignments, new cars, and any number of other things. Hating is not healthy and can take any relationship off course. Envy (hating) needs to be handled right away. Get it off of the ship right along with jealousy.

"Negativity is expensive. It costs companies millions of dollars each year," according to Gary Topchik, in *Managing Workplace Negativity*. I think of negativity as the silent killer, because it leads to negative self-talk. Once you get inside your own head, it's hard for anyone else to talk you out. Because negativity occupies so much of the mind, it is absolutely counter-productive to any relationship.

Attitude, jealousy, envy, and negativity are all cargo the relationship can do without. We must beware of detours into the wrong ports, taking on the wrong cargo, and more importantly, taking on the wrong passengers. The relationship sails best on waves of harmony. Unfortunately, the waves of harmony are not as deep as we would like. We have to recognize the position and condition that we are in, and acknowledge that some things need to be cast overboard.

Smooth Sailing

Back to our ships, even though they carry similar seed cargo, if the leadership and the followership do not sail in harmony with each other, the relationship is doomed to sink. Although the leadership and the followership can handle occasional storms and rough waters, the relationship operates best in calm, smooth waters. Close and constant attention is required to keep the relationship sailing on its proper heading.

1. **Seeds of results**
   - Either you give the people what they want, when they want it, how they want it, or they will find someone else who will understand that in business, only results really matter

2. **Seeds of trust**
   - Understand that trust is the basis of all relationships
   - Nothing will end a successful relationship faster than broken or lost trust

3. **Seeds of expectancy**
   - Understand that customers want three things, *service, agility, and cost*
     - *Service*: single point of contact, a provider who is easy to do business with, and a provider who delivers on time—every time!
     - *Agility*: available anywhere, anytime, product speed and flexibility, and total asset visibility (where is my widget?)
     - *Cost*: competitive pricing of product or service, flexible financing or special payment terms, and a single price with adjustable scheduling
   - Customers *expect* a quality product or service; *it is not a bonus you provide*
   - Fair and honest dealings with customers, employees and business partners are also expectancies

4. **Seeds of continuous improvement**
   - Customers will always be looking for new or innovative products or services
   - Customers depend on you to exceed their expectations and to surprise them with new levels of customer service

5. **Seeds of communication**
   - Always remember that successful relationships are easily lost without effective communications
   - Ensuring you provide a forum for easy, convenient customer feedback is very important to the relationship

6. **Seeds of information**
   - Keeping customers abreast of changing technologies, products and services you can provide
   - Knowledge of what changing technologies, products and services your customers desire from you

7. **Seeds of availability**
   - Being both visible and available to speak with customers and employees
   - Recognizing that it is velocity, the ability to move things faster, which will ensure growth and success in business

The three ships form a business triangle. Whether or not that triangle becomes a Bermuda Triangle is totally dependent on how well the relationships are cultivated.

The Pivot—Which Ship Leads When

Several years ago I read a story of geese that was said to be actually a lesson in teamwork. The story read, "When you see geese flying along in "V" formation, you might consider what science has discovered as to why they fly that way. As each bird flaps its wings, it creates uplift for the bird immediately following. By flying in "V" formation, the whole flock adds at least 71 percent greater flying range than if each bird flew on its own. People who share a common direction and sense of community can get where they are going more quickly and easily because they are traveling on the thrust of one another.

When a goose falls out of formation, it suddenly feels the drag and resistance of trying to go it alone—and quickly gets back into formation to take advantage of the lifting power of the bird in front. If we have as much sense as a goose, we will stay in formation with those people who are headed the same way we are.

When the head goose gets tired, it rotates back in the wing and another goose flies point. It is sensible to take turns doing demanding jobs, whether with people or with geese flying south. Geese honk from behind to encourage those up front to keep up their speed.

What messages do we give when we honk from behind? Finally—and this is important—when a goose gets sick or is wounded by gunshot, and falls out of formation, two other geese fall out with that goose and follow it down to lend help and protection. They stay with the fallen goose until it is able to fly or until it dies, and only then do they launch out on their own, or with another formation to catch up with their group.

If we have the sense of a goose, we will stand by each other like that." I really enjoy this story as it provides an excellent way to tie in the three ships together. In 1991 while still a member of the world's greatest Air Force, I was stationed at Clark Air Base, Republic of the Philippines. Depending on whom you asked, Clark was the largest overseas installation in the Air Force (some will argue that Kadena Air Base, Okinawa, Japan held that distinction). With a population well over 20,000 people, let's just say that it was a pretty big place.

The most memorable event in 1991 was the eruption of Mount Pinatubo, and the pivot positions I, and many others, found myself in. Through the damages, injuries, and loss of lives, many lessons were observed and learned. As the Vehicle Manager, my leadership skills were heavily task in devising transportation schedules for evacuation from Clark to our supposed "safe haven" at Subic Bay Naval Station, about an hour's drive to the southwest. We were staging all mission critical vehicles for follow on support once we arrived, and establishing a command center for vehicles and operators that was both safe and secure.

Very quickly, I had to pivot from the leadership to the followership and provide a sitrep (situation Report) to the senior leaders (everybody has a boss). Once the debriefings were done, it was pivot time again, as I had to engage in meetings with mid-management peers to coordinate all of our efforts for the good of the some 15,000 evacuees. This meant that the relationship was now at the front of the fleet. However, I was not the only one in pivot mode.

It wasn't long before tremendous earthquake activity left most of the buildings on Subic structurally unsound, thus unsafe. The single-story office space my team and I had taken over suddenly collapsed one early morning under the weight of volcanic ashes and heavy typhoon rains. Fortunately, some of my troops had taken the initiative to pivot from the followership to the leadership. Sensing something was about to give and in the driving wind and rain, they had taken all the essential supplies and equipment they could carry from the building to buses and trucks just short of the roof crashing in on them. Using flashlights (all electrical power had long been lost), reflective belts, and sounding off, they had saved what few radios, batteries, and our dwindling supply of MREs (meals-ready-to-eat) and water. These leaders had provided hope and opportunity for yet another day.

Just as with the geese, at some time we are all on the pivot from the front of the formation (leadership) to the back (followership), but always trying our best to support each other (relationship). The thing that impresses me is that most times, it is an instinctive rather than conscious decision to pivot. Why? Because there are no unimportant jobs on either ship, and any person who feels they have an unimportant job, must be a stowaway.

Relationship Seeds Summary

Poet Pablo Neruda penned, "When I see the sea once more, will the sea have seen or not seen me?" How many times has a neglected party in a relationship wondered if you have seen or not seen them . . . literally? Relationships must be continuously cultivated if they are to stay healthy and grow. How important are relationships to you? Do you stand on the docks and wait for your ship to come in, or do you dive in from the docks to swim out and meet it? Which, do you think, is most appreciated?

Section 3 Review: Chapters 7, 8, and 9

The Seed: Leadership, Followership, & Relationship

1. The author likens an organization to a garden and states every garden has weeds. Why do some leaders have trouble cultivating weeds from the organizational garden?

   _____
   _____
   _____
   _____

2. What is a "gap analysis" and what is its importance to an organization?

   _____
   _____
   _____
   _____

3. Why is candor an asset to a leader?

   _____
   _____
   _____
   _____

4. The author states as a society, we have lost our capacity to dream and create. Why is this detrimental?

   _____
   _____
   _____
   _____

5. On the followership, attitudes are a secret power working twenty-four hours a day, for good or bad. Give an example of a way in which this may be bad.

   _____
   _____
   _____

6. In The Battle of Two Wolves, the old Cherokee Chief talks of a battle between good and evil. Discuss a relationship battle going on inside of you and which side you are feeding.

   _____
   _____
   _____

7. Identify the two most dangerous cargo carried on the relationship and what actions you should take in troubled waters.

   _____
   _____
   _____

8. What is the silent killer that gets inside your head and why is it then so hard to stop?

   _____
   _____
   _____

FINAL THOUGHTS

Putting It All Together

When sailing independent of each other, the ***3-Ships of Success, leadership, followership, and relationship*** can bring limited, short-range success. However, when these three ship sail in unison, they form a powerful armada of long-term success. We all know of powerful leaders who have great success for a while, then fall from grace if the followership veers off course, or if an act of negativity fires a shot across the bow of the relationship. Another great truth that I have heard is that you can tell the character of a man by the way he treats those who can do absolutely nothing for him. I think this can be a great lesson for any leader.

    On the followership, remember the importance of having a plan and a purpose. At some point in time, the door of opportunity is going to open for you. If you have prepared yourself and you are eligible, you have a choice. The consequence of your choice determines your path. It has been said when things get tough at work, you have one of two choices. You can say, "Oh hell" and get cranky, or you can say, "Oh well" and get cracking. I usually say, "Well hell," and find the best way to make it happen. Old rules from the past ("Don't ask questions, just do what I tell you.") don't work well in today's environment. "Just do it" works well as the Nike slogan, but has a negative effect in today's business environment. Today's followers are too smart, and too hungry for their own success to adhere to a "Just do it" mandate. Today, my way or the highway is often not a threat, but a challenge. Results, trust, expectancy, continuous improvement, communication, information, and availability will calm the waters of success for smooth sailing and keeping all three ships in shipshape. To paraphrase former Secretary of State **Colin**

Powell, lead from the windshield, not from the rearview mirror. Get away from old ways of doing things by staying "in the moment."

In reality, the relationship is the biggest ship in the fleet. The smoother the relationships, the smoother the business. Sink the relationship, sink the business. It's just that simple. Relationships are the logistics keys of any business, and there is one simple rule to logistics; you don't need it, until you need it, and then you need it. If you want to have a successful relationship, make it a reciprocal, feel good relationship. Keep both parties feeling good, and you keep a good relationship. Plan your voyage early. Plot out what you can, can't, will, won't, might or try to do. Make your customers feel welcome, important, and valued. To aid you in your quest for success, I offer you these powerful words from Gerard Hargraves:

Did is a word of achievement
Won't is a word of defeat
Might is a word of bereavement
Can't is a word of defeat

Ought is a word of duty
Try is the word of the hour
Will is a word of beauty
Can is a word of power

All the best and nothing but success is my wish for you. Sail on!

AN INVITATION

"I not only use all the brains I have, but all I can borrow."
—*Woodrow Wilson*

If you have stories or thoughts on how the Ships of Success impact your business or personal life, I would love to hear them. Please write, email, or fax them to me. I also teach customer service workshops, so keep me in mind for your training needs or refer me to someone else in need. If you do, I will provide you a gift copy of my award winning book, ***Management Out of the Blue***, either hard copy or audio CD.

Burton's Training Accents
P.O. Box 2126
Waldorf, MD 20601
Phone: 301 751-2694
Fax: 301 856-8580
Email: admin@burtonstrainingaccent.com

A FEW THINGS ABOUT THE AUTHOR...

MacArthur Burton is President & Chief Executive Officer of Burton's Training Accents!, Incorporated (LLC), which is a minority owned speaking/consulting/training/coaching & mentoring business, focused on organizations within the federal, state, and local government. Training Accents is based in Waldorf, Maryland. **Mr. Burton**'s company is dedicated to enlighten, encourage, and empower people to discover and unleash their true talents, share their God given gifts and improve their quality of life personally and professionally.

He is the author of "***Management Out of the Blue***," which won the coveted Editor's Choice Award from iUniverse, Inc. The stories are written in an easy to read, humorous, one-page format that offer insight to different ways of dealing with work place situations. Each story ends with a challenge to the reader to "Think about it" in terms of how they deal with both internal and external customers. He has also authored numerous newspaper articles, which were published here in the U.S. and in Europe.

Mr. Burton has over 20 years experience in the public speaking arena, both in the military and in the private sector. He joined Toastmasters International in 1999 where he studied under the direction of some of the finest motivational and inspirational speakers in the world. Through dedication and hard work, he has achieved the status of Distinguished Toastmaster, the highest rating within Toastmasters. He has completed a 30 year career in the United States Air Force, worked for General Motors Corporation as a Production Manager, and the Department of Defense Civil Service Commission.

Mr. Burton earned a Masters degree in Human Relations from the University of Oklahoma, and a Bachelors degree in Business and Management from the University of Maryland. His passions, building trust relationships and positive communications, have inspired the minds, hearts, and actions of women, men, and youth nationwide to greatly improve interpersonal communications in their lives professionally and personally. Additionally, he has a love for inspirational poetry. His recent poem, "***I Blame No One But Me***," was recognized by the International Society of Poets with their Editor's Choice Award.

REFERENCES

Hill, N. (1960). <u>Think & Grow Rich</u>. New York, N.Y.: Random House Publishing Group.

Winget, L. (2007). <u>It's Called Work for a Reason.</u> New York, N.Y.: Gotham Books

Jolles, R.L. (1993, 2003, 2005). <u>How to Run Seminars & Workshops</u>. Hoboken, N.Y.: John Wiley & Sons, Inc.

Thomas, P.W. (2005). <u>Power Steps: Ten Principles of Success</u>. Brookeville, MD.: Success Behavior Institute.

Burton, M. (2005). <u>Management Out of the Blue</u>. Lincoln, NE.: iUniverse, Inc.

Jolley, W. (1997). <u>It Only Takes A Minute To Change Your Life</u>. New York, N.Y.: St. Martin's Press.

Bergren, M., Cox, M., Detmar, J. (2002). <u>Improvise This!</u> New York, N.Y.: Hyperion Books.

Olsen, Jeff. (2011) <u>The Slight Edge Audio Book</u>. Momentum Media, Video Plus, LP.

Covey, Stephen R. (1989). <u>The 7-Habits of Highly Effective People</u>. London, UK: Simon & Schuster UK, Ltd

www.ingramcontent.com/pod-product-compliance
Lightning Source LLC
Chambersburg PA
CBHW021004180526
45163CB00005B/1886